ENGINEERING THE HUMAN BODY

EXOSKELETONS

Tammy Gagne

FOCUS
READERS

NAVIGATOR

Focus Readers is distributed by North Star Editions:
sales@northstareditions.com | 888-417-0195

Produced for Focus Readers by Red Line Editorial.

Content Consultant: Richard Weir, Research Associate Professor of Bioengineering, University of Colorado, Denver

Photographs ©: Salvatore di Nolfi/Keystone/AP Images, cover, 1; Jelena Danilovic/iStockphoto, 4–5; chudakov2/iStockphoto, 7, 9; Rob Carty/US Army/AB Forces News Collection/Alamy, 10–11; count_kert/iStockphoto, 13; Amelie-Benoist/BSIP SA/Alamy, 15; dpa picture alliance archive/Alamy, 17; Vereshchagin Dmitry/Shutterstock Images, 18–19; Alexander Drago/Reuters/Newscom, 21; Monkey Business Images/Shutterstock Images, 23; Erik Tham/EThamPhoto/Alamy, 24–25; Jim West/Alamy, 27; AnneCordon/iStockphoto, 29

Library of Congress Cataloging-in-Publication Data
Names: Gagne, Tammy, author.
Title: Exoskeletons / by Tammy Gagne.
Description: Lake Elmo, MN : Focus Readers, 2020. | Series: Engineering the human body | Audience: Grades 4 to 6. | Includes bibliographical references and index.
Identifiers: LCCN 2019002986 (print) | LCCN 2019006125 (ebook) | ISBN 9781641859707 (pdf) | ISBN 9781641859011 (e-book) | ISBN 9781641857635 (hardcover) | ISBN 9781641858328 (pbk.)
Subjects: LCSH: Prosthesis--Juvenile literature. | Human skeleton--Juvenile literature. | Robotics in medicine--Juvenile literature. | Medical technology--Juvenile literature. | Medical innovations--Juvenile literature.
Classification: LCC RD130 (ebook) | LCC RD130 .G3445 2020 (print) | DDC 617.9/56--dc23
LC record available at https://lccn.loc.gov/2019002986

Printed in the United States of America
Mankato, MN
May, 2019

ABOUT THE AUTHOR

Tammy Gagne has written more than 200 books for both adults and children. She resides in northern New England with her husband and son. Her most recent titles include *Artificial Organs* and *Extra Senses*.

TABLE OF CONTENTS

CHAPTER 1

FROM PARALYSIS TO MOVEMENT

In 2004, Steven Sanchez fell off his BMX bike. The accident **paralyzed** him instantly. Afterward, he used a wheelchair to get around. But today, Sanchez can walk again. He moves with the help of an exoskeleton.

This device is a machine that a person wears. The prefix *exo-* means "outside."

People who are paralyzed from the waist down can use wheelchairs to move around.

So, an exoskeleton is a skeleton. But it goes outside the body. Different models have different uses.

The model Sanchez uses is called the Phoenix. He wears the metal frame over his lower body. He also holds crutches. He presses buttons on the crutches. The buttons control motors attached to the frame. The motors move his legs. Sanchez wears a backpack, too. Inside is a battery that powers the machine.

Sanchez had to learn how to use the device. But in less than an hour, he could walk with slow, careful steps. Sanchez was one of the first people to test the model. Today, other people can buy it.

Crutches support the user as he or she walks with an exoskeleton.

But exoskeletons are very expensive. And although many companies are developing exoskeletons, the devices are not widely available yet.

Companies hope these devices will help future users. Some models are being designed to help people with disabilities.

These devices could help users move their arms or legs. They could help users get exercise. The devices could also help users with daily tasks. Users could stand and take slow steps.

Other models are being designed to help **stroke** patients. After a stroke,

STRONGER AND FASTER

Certain jobs require heavy lifting. For these jobs, some workers could use exoskeletons. They could wear the devices and lift objects safely. Workers could lift objects for longer periods of time. Also, users could get more work done in a day. A strong person might lift 200 pounds (91 kg) once or twice. Then he or she would need to rest. But with an exoskeleton, a person could lift this weight all day.

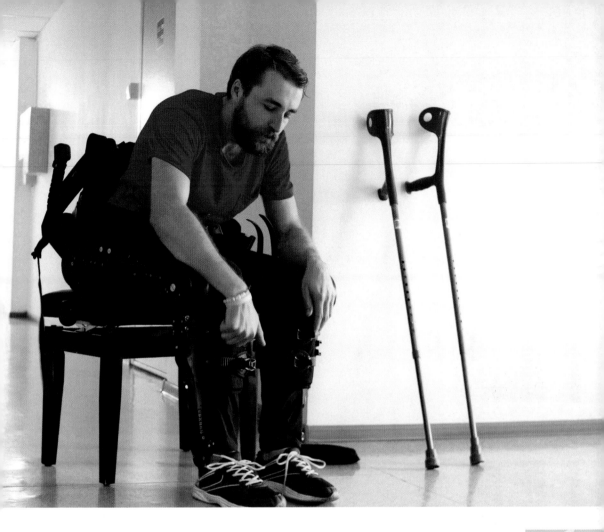

A user straps his legs into his exoskeleton.

patients might have trouble moving their arms. They may even become paralyzed. Exoskeletons could help some stroke patients regain movement in their arms.

CHAPTER 2

DEVELOPING THE TECHNOLOGY

Soldiers often have to carry heavy gear. The US military thought exoskeletons could help. Soldiers hoped the devices would save time and energy. Engineers built the first models in the 1960s. But these early models were bulky and heavy. For example, one model weighed 1,500 pounds (680 kg).

A soldier tries out a new exoskeleton to help him walk longer distances and carry heavier gear.

Companies began designing their own models in the late 1960s. Many focused on helping people with paralysis. Being paralyzed affects more than a person's body. It can also affect a person's mental health. Many activities require standing or walking. Having to sit still all the time can lead to boredom. Not being able to move can also be upsetting. It can even cause **depression**.

People with paralysis often use wheelchairs to get around. The first models did not have motors. People moved the wheels with their hands. But even motorized wheelchairs come with problems. For instance, they create a

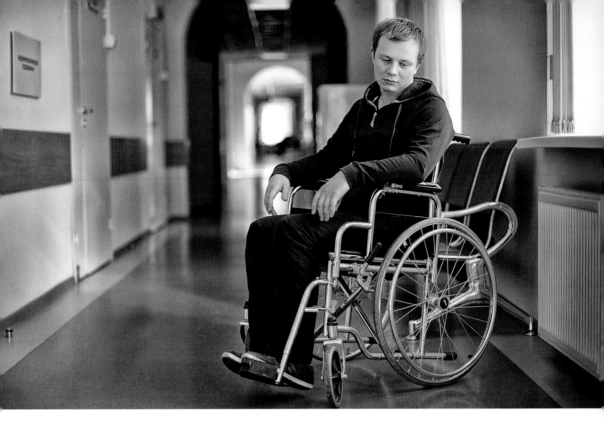

People who are used to an active lifestyle may experience depression after becoming paralyzed.

height difference between the user and other people. Exoskeletons could solve this problem.

In the late 1990s, a Japanese company created a new model called HAL. This device helped paralyzed people stand.

It moved their legs. By 2013, the company had created a full-body exoskeleton known as HAL 5. The whole device weighed only 22 pounds (10 kg).

Companies continue to develop exoskeleton technology. Some are focusing on **rehabilitation** devices.

REDUCING PAIN

People with paralysis do not have a sense of touch in their paralyzed limbs. But many patients can still feel pain in those limbs. Patients often describe it as a burning feeling. Using an exoskeleton has been shown to reduce this common problem. Doctors believe the exoskeleton tricks the brain. The brain thinks that the limb is working normally.

Exoskeletons could help patients recover after a stroke or head injury.

After an injury, some patients need physical therapy. It helps them regain the movement they had before the injury. Exoskeletons could be part of this therapy. They could help people exercise their limbs.

EXOSKELETONS

An exoskeleton is a robotic frame. It fits over the user's body. When the frame moves, the person also moves. But the frame performs most of the work. Users must practice using an exoskeleton. It takes time to learn to use the machine.

Many exoskeletons are made of metal. Others contain certain types of fabric. This material makes the exoskeleton more **flexible**. Some models even contain **sensors**. The sensors help the device respond to the user's movements. In one system, a user leans on a pair of crutches. The user shifts his or her weight forward. The device senses that the user wants to take a step. The device moves. It lifts the user's leg and takes a step.

Exoskeletons require a power source. But creating long-lasting batteries is a challenge.

Batteries must be lightweight. They also must be small enough to fit inside a backpack. Big batteries are not easy for users to carry around all day.

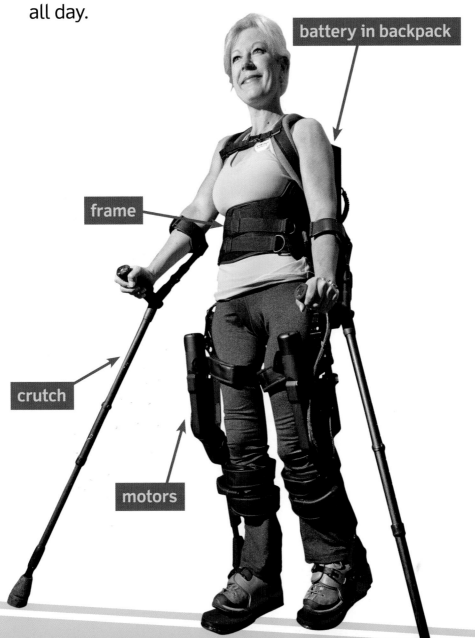

battery in backpack

frame

crutch

motors

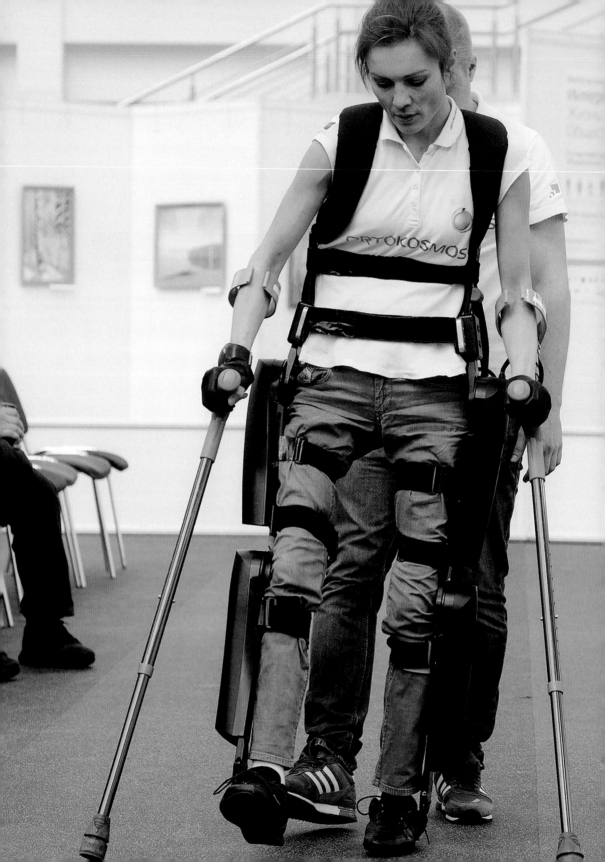

CHAPTER 3

EXOSKELETONS TODAY

Many companies are developing and testing exoskeletons. Some models could help people who have medical conditions. The eLegs device is one example. Users move the crutches. From this motion, the device senses how the user wants to move. The exoskeleton responds by moving.

A woman takes slow steps in her exoskeleton.

Other models could help people with lifting. For example, one company built an exoskeleton with a carbon fiber motor. This material is very lightweight. The entire model weighs only 13 pounds (6 kg). But it can help the user lift up to 33 pounds (15 kg). The model includes sensors. They detect when a person lifts or carries an object. The motor turns on only when it senses this activity.

Military models need to lift even more weight. The BLEEX model is fairly heavy. But it allows soldiers to carry more than 200 pounds (91 kg) in a backpack.

The HULC is another model used for carrying heavy loads. The HULC can carry

Exoskeletons are becoming more lightweight as the technology develops.

the same amount of weight as the BLEEX.

But it works on any type of **terrain**.

Carrying objects on hills is much harder

than carrying objects on flat ground.

The model is also very strong and flexible. Users can crawl. They can do other complex movements, too.

One challenge is work that requires **precision**. Picking up small objects is not easy for most robotic hands. Putting objects down in an exact location can also be difficult. However, one company claims its Guardian XO model has solved this problem. This model is just as strong as the others being made today. But it can perform highly precise tasks that most models cannot.

Designing a device that can walk is not an easy task. The machine must be able to **mimic** a human's gait. A gait is the way

A person's gait changes as he or she gets older.

a person walks. It includes the speed and the length of each step. Even the way a person sets down his or her foot affects gait. Engineers design exoskeletons to copy these movements. But the result is still different from a natural gait.

CHAPTER 4

THE FUTURE OF EXOSKELETONS

More people will use exoskeletons in the future. One company predicts that these devices will be part of everyday life by the mid-2030s. Cost will play a big role in this change. The machines will become more affordable over time.

One day, governments may be able to give exoskeletons to emergency workers.

As costs go down, more people will be able to use exoskeletons to walk again.

Firefighters could use the devices to carry gear. EMTs and nurses could use them to move patients. Having the machines' help with lifting will make these jobs safer.

Making things safer is good for people. It is also good for the economy. When a worker gets hurt, the employer has to pay for medical treatment. Heavy lifting is one of the top causes of workplace injuries. US businesses spend a combined $15 billion each year because of these injuries. Companies could invest in exoskeletons to lower this cost.

In the future, exoskeletons will be used more often in rehabilitation. Currently, most patients travel to medical offices

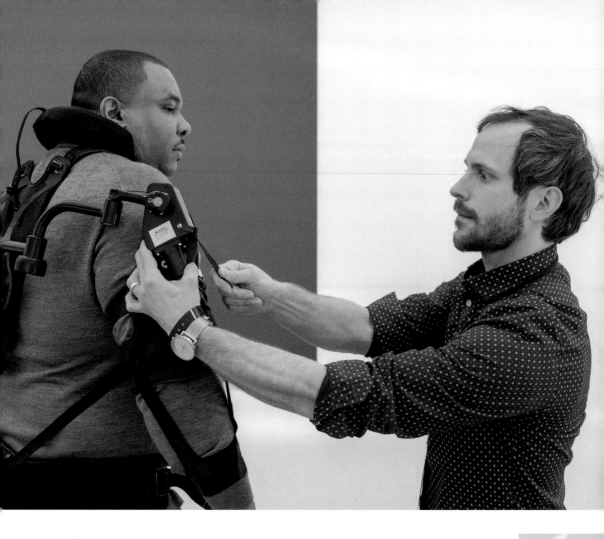

This exoskeleton is designed to help workers perform repetitive tasks without injuring themselves.

for physical therapy. Patients with their own devices could do therapy at home instead. The use of the devices could also speed up recovery times.

Exoskeletons are not helpful without a power source. For this reason, engineers are searching for new energy sources. They are developing models that could run off hydrogen fuel. Future users might stop at hydrogen refueling stations to power up.

MIND-CONTROLLED DEVICES

Mind control might sound like science fiction. But scientists are now developing exoskeletons with this feature. These models will receive signals from the user's brain. They will sense which way the user wants to move. It will take time before these models are ready for use. But experts are confident that one day these models will be available.

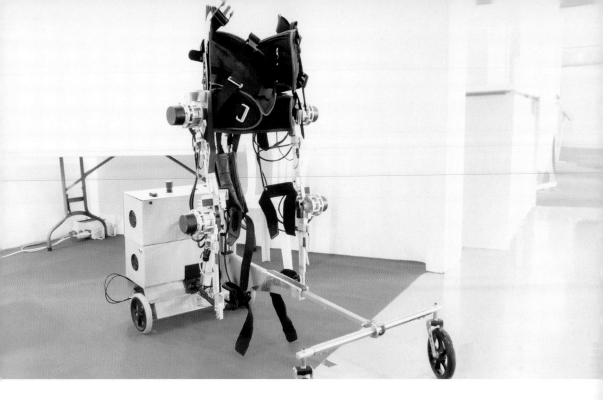

Exoskeletons are becoming more common in physical therapy and in the workplace.

Exoskeletons could even be used for space exploration. Space suits are heavy. A suit that can move itself could be helpful. As the technology develops, researchers will find new uses for these devices. They will find new ways for exoskeletons to improve human life.

FOCUS ON
EXOSKELETONS

Write your answers on a separate piece of paper.

1. Write a paragraph summarizing the main ideas from Chapter 1.

2. If you had a job that involved heavy lifting, would you be willing to learn how to use an exoskeleton? Why or why not?

3. Which exoskeleton is most successful at precise tasks?
   A. HAL
   B. Guardian XO
   C. HULC

4. Why might HULC be considered an improvement over the BLEEX model?
   A. HULC weighs less than BLEEX.
   B. HULC can carry more weight than BLEEX.
   C. HULC can work on a variety of terrains.

Answer key on page 32.

GLOSSARY

depression
A medical condition of deep, long-lasting sadness or loss of interest.

flexible
Easy to bend or change.

mimic
To copy an appearance or behavior.

paralyzed
Caused part of the body to become incapable of movement.

precision
The quality of being extremely precise and exact.

rehabilitation
The process of restoring movement and other abilities following an injury.

sensors
Devices that detect things, such as movement.

stroke
A disease that occurs when blood flow to an area of the brain is blocked.

terrain
The physical features of an area of land.

TO LEARN MORE

BOOKS

Howell, Izzi. *Robots*. North Mankato, MN: Capstone Press, 2019.

Hulick, Kathryn. *Medical Robots*. Minneapolis: Abdo Publishing, 2019.

Mooney, Carla. *Wearable Robots*. Chicago: Norwood House Press, 2017.

NOTE TO EDUCATORS

Visit **www.focusreaders.com** to find lesson plans, activities, links, and other resources related to this title.

INDEX

Answer Key: 1. Answers will vary; 2. Answers will vary; 3. B; 4. C